YOUR LAND
AND
MY LAND
AFRICA

We Visit

GHANA

John

Bankston

Mitchell Lane

PUBLISHERS
P.O. Box 196
Hockessin, Delaware 19707

YOUR LAND
AND
MY LAND
AFRICA

Egypt
Ethiopia
Ghana
Kenya
Libya
Madagascar
Morocco
Nigeria
Rwanda
South Africa

LIBYA

EGYPT

Aswān

YOUR LAND AND MY LAND AFRICA

We Visit
GHANA

SUDAN

Addis
Ababa

Gulf of Aden

Mitchell Lane
PUBLISHERS

Printing   1   2   3   4   5   6   7   8   9

Library of Congress Cataloging-in-Publication Data
Bankston, John, 1974-
  We visit Ghana / by John Bankston.
      p. cm. — (Your land and my land. Africa)
  Includes bibliographical references and index.
  ISBN 978-1-61228-303-6 (library bound)
  1. Ghana—Juvenile literature. I. Title. II. Series: Your land and my land (Mitchell Lane Publishers). Africa.
  DT510.B36 2013
  966.7—dc23
                                                    2012041970
eBook ISBN: 9781612283777

PUBLISHER'S NOTE: This story is based on the author's extensive research, which he believes to be accurate. Documentation of this research is on page 61.

The internet sites referenced herein were active as of the publication date. Due to the fleeting nature of some websites, we cannot guarantee they will all be active when you are reading this book.

PLB

Contents

Introduction

Ghana is a trendsetter. The West African country led the continent through centuries of change. Across Africa, countries endured bloody wars for independence, the destruction of land, and widespread poverty. Yet Africa is also home to startlingly beautiful landscapes and some of the rarest animals on earth. Governments from coast to coast have recently begun protecting these vital resources.

At one time, nearly every country in Africa was run by outsiders. Decisions affecting the lives of Africans were made thousands of miles away in places like Britain, Spain, and Portugal.

Lying in West Africa, and south of the enormous Sahara Desert, Ghana is almost midway between the countries of Senegal and Cameroon. Bordered on the south by the Atlantic Ocean, Ghana shares its borders with Togo to the east, the Ivory Coast to the west, and Burkina Faso to the north.

Today there are fifty-seven independent countries in Africa. Ghana was the first of the sub-Saharan colonies to become independent. For over a century, Ghanaians fought small and large battles to put an end to Britain's colonial rule. Just as the United States declared its independence from Britain in 1776, Ghana declared its own freedom in 1957. Following Ghana's achievement of independence, it gained numerous advantages. The central regions produced enough food to feed its people, and offered ample exports as well. Precious minerals provided another source of revenue.

Ghana's Volta Region

GHANA

AFRICA

Yet like many other countries across the continent, Ghana endured various leaders who resisted free elections, trying to stay in power for life. It also suffered political unrest as members of the military forced these presidents out of office.

Ghana's resources were plundered. Forests torn down for farm land increased soil erosion and flooding. The damage led to huge losses of crops. Decades after independence, many Ghanaians faced hunger and poverty, and had few opportunities to improve their lives.

Yet just as Ghana was a leader among African countries seeking freedom, today the country stands as an example for any nation that hopes to preserve its resources while increasing its wealth. Ghana introduced the first economic recovery program in Africa. Businesses once mismanaged by the state were sold. Privately run companies began making money. Meanwhile, as the country became safer and more stable, it worked to attract visitors.

Tourists spend money. Some of the money they spend maintains wilderness areas. Over 14 percent of Ghana's land is now protected. Inside these wilderness parks, the forests are returning. Endangered animals run free. Today Ghana faces numerous challenges, yet it remains a shining example for other countries seeking to improve.

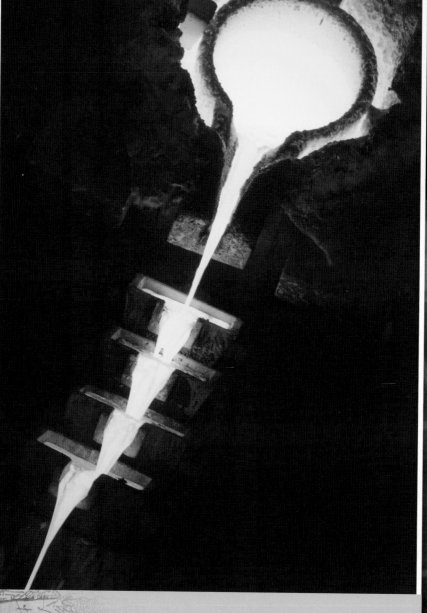

Ghana is known worldwide for its gold. The Obuasi Mine, now owned by AngloGold Ashanti, has been producing gold since 1897.

Welcome to Ghana!

You might be surprised to know that Ghana has been one of the world's largest producers of gold for hundreds of years. This precious metal attracted the attention of Europeans who quickly colonized the region. They called it the "Gold Coast."

Today, Ghana is home to one of the largest gold mines in the world. The Obuasi Gold Mine in the Ashanti Region has been producing gold since 1897.

Hot and humid like most tropical countries near the equator, Ghana is slightly smaller than the state of Oregon. Most of the country has two rainy seasons, from April to June and from September to November. In the north, the rainy season lasts from April to September. From November to February, people living in northern Ghana face the Harmattan. These hot winds blowing in from the Sahara coat the region in red dust.

Most of the country is fairly flat, although the Akwapim Mountain Range has several peaks that soar to over 2,000 feet (600 meters). Mount Afadjato is over 2,900 feet (880 meters) high.

Picturing Africa, many people imagine dry, grassy areas filled with exotic animals. Ghana's savanna region fits that image most closely. Lying in the northern and coastal parts of the country, these areas receive less rainfall than the other portions of the country. In the north the grass can grow 10 feet (3 meters) high, while trees are spread far apart. Few people live in this area.

Lake Volta

The southeastern edges of the savanna are dominated by Lake Volta and its connecting rivers. Created when the Akosombo Dam blocked the flow of the Volta River, it is the largest artificial lake in the world with a surface area of over 3,200 square miles (8,500 square kilometers).

Along the southern end of Lake Volta is the Kwahu Plateau. Running from northwest to southeast, the plateau separates the North's dry savanna from the forests of the South. The coastal areas meet the Gulf of Guinea, and boast marshes, swamps, and numerous lagoons.

Ghana still lives up to its Gold Coast name. Gold is mined far from its coast—including in the northern forests. Almost half of the country's income from exports comes from gold production. Still, farmers throughout the country produce a variety of goods including peanuts, sugarcane, yams, and rice. Ghana's biggest agricultural export is cocoa. In the 1960s, Ghana produced over one-third of all the cocoa in the world. Today the country exports over 1.1 million tons (1 million metric tons) of cocoa every year. Since cocoa is a prime candy ingredient, Ghana could also be called "The Chocolate Coast."

FYI FACT:

Surf's Up! Along the southernmost tip of Ghana's coast, Dixcove offers surfers some of the best waves in the country.

WHERE IN THE WORLD IS GHANA?

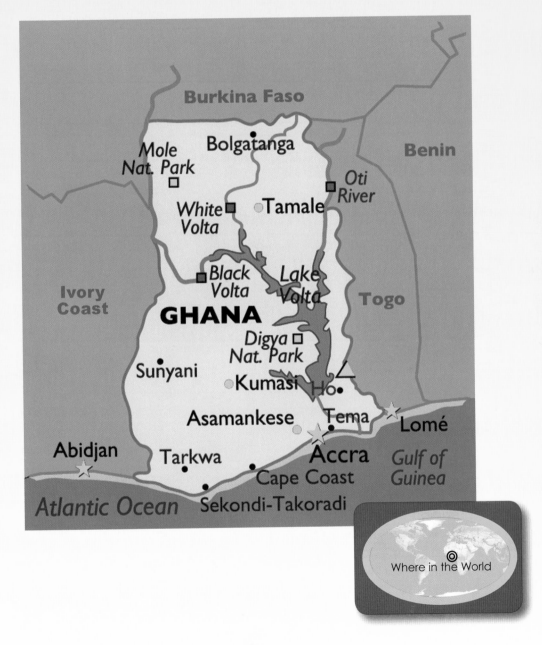

Burkina Faso

Benin

Mole
Nat. Park

Bolgatanga

Oti
River

White
Volta

Tamale

Ivory
Coast

Black
Volta

Lake
Volta

Togo

GHANA

Digya □
Nat. Park

Sunyani

Kumasi

Ho

Asamankese

Tema

Lomé

Abidjan

Tarkwa

Accra

Gulf of
Guinea

Cape Coast

Atlantic Ocean

Sekondi-Takoradi

Where in the World

The remains from a town abandoned because of desertification.

GHANA FACTS AT A GLANCE

Ghanaian Flag

Full name: Republic of Ghana
Official language: English
Population: 25,241,998 (2012 estimate)
Land area: 87,851 square miles (227,533 square kilometers); slightly smaller than Oregon
Capital: Accra
Government: Constitutional Democracy
Ethnic makeup: Akan 45.3%, Mole-Dagbon 15.2%, Ewe 11.7%, Ga-Dangme 7.3%, Guan 4%, Gurma 3.6%, Grusi 2.6%, Mandé-Busanga 1%, other tribes 1.4%, other 7.8%
Religions: Christian 68.8% (Pentecostal/Charismatic 24.1%, Protestant 18.6%, Catholic 15.1%, other 11%), Muslim 15.9%, traditional 8.5%, other 0.7%, none 6.1%
Exports: Gold, cocoa, timber, tuna, bauxite, aluminum, manganese ore, diamonds, horticulture
Imports: Capital equipment, petroleum, food
Crops: Cocoa, rice, cassava (yuca), peanuts, corn, shea nuts, bananas
Average high temperatures:
    Accra: February 88°F (31°C); August 80°F (27°C)
    Tamale: February 99°F (37°C); August 84°F (29°C)
Average annual rainfall:
    Accra: 28.5 inches (72.5 centimeters)
    Tamale: 41 inches (104.5 centimeters)
Highest point: Mount Afadjato—2,904 feet (885 meters)
Longest river: Volta River, which has three branches—the Red, Black, and White Volta Rivers—they total approximately 1,000 miles (1,600 kilometers)
Flag: Three equal horizontal bands of red (top), yellow, and green, with a large black five-pointed star centered in the yellow band; red symbolizes the blood shed for independence, yellow represents the country's mineral wealth, while green stands for its forests and natural wealth; the black star is said to be the lodestar of African freedom.
National sport: Football (soccer)

Source: *CIA World Factbook:* Ghana

Perched over 100 feet in the air, the canopy walks at Kakum National Park offer visitors a "bird's eye view" of the park.

Where the Wild Things Are

Exploring Kakum National Park, it is easy to be scared. The scenery is beautiful. The park features an abundance of native African animals, living in the wild without the cages typically found in a zoo. The frightening part for many visitors is in how the scenery is viewed.

Canopy walkways crisscross the preserve. Similar to a small wooden bridge, the walkways creak and groan, moving with the breeze and whenever another tourist nervously leaves the relative safety of small viewing platforms. Encircling trees, the platforms interrupt the walkways which stretch for over 1,000 feet (300 meters) across the park.

Along the walkways, tourists step slowly and awkwardly onto planks barely wider than an adult's shoulders. Overhead, wires and thick netting connect the canopies to sturdy trees. Just above eye level are the treetops, where all manner of animals from birds to monkeys make their homes. Over 130 feet (40 meters) below? Solid ground awaits.

About 12 miles (19 kilometers) from the town of Cape Coast and the Gulf of Guinea, Kakum National Park lies in Ghana's Central Region along the southern portion of the country. Abundant rainfall produces dense rainforests for over 150 miles (240 kilometers) inland. For visitors, the canopy walkway offers the courageous a view that is truly "bird's eye." It also makes it harder to get lost.

"No living system on the terrestrial Earth is as diverse as a tropical rainforest," asserts John Reader. "Many of the trees look alike and have similarly-shaped laurel-like leaves with 'drip-tips,' but in fact almost every tree found in the forest is likely to be a different species." In just 12 acres (5 hectares) there might be 200 different species of large trees. "[The tropical rainforest] even makes its own weather: water vapour rising from the forest forms massive banks of cloud, and the rain they eventually release falls right back on the forest itself."[1]

Beneath the canopy walks, lush vegetation shelters elephants, monkeys, and antelopes. The exotic live beside the ordinary, as insects survive below ground, while overhead are numerous birds and many of the 400 different species of butterflies inhabiting the park—including

Four hundred different species of butterfly call Kakum National Park home, including this female African swallowtail.

giant African swallowtails with wingspans over 8 inches (20 centimeters) across!

Duikers—a form of antelope—stride across the numerous protected parks of Ghana. This family includes the yellow-backed duiker which usually sports a yellow patch on its back and Maxwell's duiker which has white markings on its face.

Although today the land is protected, a few decades ago, the rainforests of Kakum were almost destroyed. Across the world, more and more people need places to live, work, and farm. Their needs often conflict with those of other species. Usually humans win. Trees are chopped down with axes and chainsaws, fields are paved over. Eventually, the shadows of buildings replace the dark canopies of forests. With each new town and city, more species vanish, dying off and becoming extinct—disappearing from our world forever.

In Africa, the destruction of trees has led to increased desertification —as land once rich in plant life becomes a desert. The United Nations, an international body of nations set up in 1945 to promote world peace, counts Ghana as one of forty-one African countries fighting to reverse this dangerous process. "When people live in poverty, they have little choice but to over-exploit the land," a United Nations report explains. "When the land eventually becomes uneconomic to farm, these people are often forced into internal and cross-border migrations... Food security can ultimately be put at risk when people already living on the edge face severe droughts and other environmental disasters."[2]

In a report detailing Ghana's challenges, Edward M. Telly admitted that when a country tries to grow—providing homes, jobs, and farms— "the process of development has often left in its trail, deterioration of productive lands, deforestation, desertification, air and water pollution."[3]

To combat this, Ghana established the Environmental Protection Agency in 1994. The country wants to ensure that environmental protection is a main priority in future development. Numerous programs have been created in Ghana to protect wilderness areas like

FYI FACT:

Mole National Park has two elephants who enjoy posing for pictures with people. One of these elephants, "Action," is famous for occasionally trumpeting loudly during a photo. Visitors who realize that elephants usually trumpet as a sign of anger or nervousness often race to their vehicles, but Action evidently does this just for fun.

Kakum National Park. The Natural Resources Management Programme hopes to "protect, rehabilitate, and sustainably manage national land, forest, savanna woodlands, and wildlife resources and to sustainably increase the income of rural communities who own these resources."[4]

Established in 1960, Kakum National Park now provides the only skywalk tours in all of Africa. It is just one of sixteen protected parks and reserves in the country along with five coastal wetlands. One protected area, the Boabeng-Fiema Monkey Sanctuary, protects the black-and-white colobus monkey, a jet black monkey known for its white facial markings and ability to leap up to 50 feet (15 meters). It is also home to the Lowe's mona monkey, noted for the stripe over its eye.

Hippos can be seen in several parks, including the Bui National Park. Set along a protected area of the Black Volta River, this park is also home to numerous antelopes and monkeys.

The largest nature preserve in Ghana, Mole National Park stretches over 1,800 square miles (4,800 square kilometers) in the northern part of the country. Boasting over ninety different species of mammals, the park offers visitors a chance to see many animals including baboons, hyenas, and buffalo. Some of the park's residents are harder to spot, like its small number of leopards and lions. Still, most visitors get to see the park's abundant antelopes, monkeys, and crocodiles along with some of Mole National's 500 to 800 elephants.

Elephants have an unlikely, if distant, relative. Across Ghana the rock hyrax is often seen sunning itself on the rocks. Although its teeth resemble an elephant's tusks, it looks like a large guinea pig. The rock

With over 500 elephants living within its borders, Mole National Park offers visitors plentiful opportunities for pictures.

hyrax weighs less than 10 pounds (5 kilograms). Like elephants, rock hyraxes have a well-developed sense of hearing, excellent memory, and toenails. Scientists believe that rock hyraxes and elephants shared a common ancestor as many as 50 million years ago.

One creature visitors don't have to go to a park to see is the house gecko. With their bug-eyes, many people find these harmless insect eaters to be pretty cute. This species of lizard can be found in many of the hotels and homes in Ghana.

Across Ghana, tourists and locals alike shop at roadside stands for goods like apples, palm oil, and pineapples.

Across Ghana, small roadside stands and shops offer everything from wooden toys, beads, and drums to pots for the kitchen and freshly baked bread. Family-run weaving centers offer traditional clothing made from world-famous kente cloth while street peddlers offer rice and stew from containers balanced on their heads. Entire villages are known for specializing in a particular craft.

Ghana is predominantly rural. The two cities with the most people, Accra (the capital) and Kumasi, both have populations in the millions, yet retain a feel of smaller towns with open air markets which combine bustling crowds and a variety of items for sale. Many of these crafts and food are produced as they have been for hundreds, even thousands of years.

Ancient crafts tie Ghanaians to their ancestors. Most of them still live on farms or in small villages. English is Ghana's official language, but most Ghanaians still speak one of many languages that their ancestors spoke. Gur speakers originally settled in the dry, savanna regions of the North, while Kwa speakers lived in the southern rainforests and along the coast. The Ewe-speaking people lived in the southern portions of the Volta Region. Each of these language groups have split into multiple modern languages today.

Akan is a Kwa language spoken by the country's largest ethnic group, the Akan people. These people dominate the densely-populated southern regions and represent some 45 percent of the population. Ghana has over one hundred different ethnic groups who speak more than fifty different languages. But all of them are related to the first human beings, whom scientists believe first lived in Africa.

Ghana is a small country within an enormous continent. Africa could comfortably contain the United States and still have plenty of room for India, China, and Argentina. Ghana rests on the continent's bulge, part of the West African craton. Cratons are large, stable portions of rock that extend below the earth's crust into the mantle.

All of Africa is quite old, but the West African craton is even older. Formed approximately 2 billion years ago, it is one of the oldest land masses in the world. Like most ancient terrain, the surface has been worn down over time. Erosion from coastal tides, ice, and wind have left the region fairly flat.

Most scientists believe that the earliest humans lived more than 5 million years ago. These humans lived in East Africa, in and around the modern countries of Kenya and Tanzania, far from Ghana. Short and covered in hair, these early humans, called hominids, looked more like apes than people. But they evolved. Changing slowly over time and adapting to the East African environment, they developed tools and formed communities. About 200,000 years ago, they evolved into modern people or *Homo sapiens* (which means literally, "wise man.")

Homo sapiens began leaving their African home for Asia and Arabia some 100,000 years ago. Forty thousand years ago they reached Europe and Australia; by 30,000 years ago, they had arrived in East Asia. Around 14,000 years ago, some of them crossed into North America. Every one of these early humans could trace their origins to the continent of Africa. In fact, scientists believe we all can do this.

Geneticists are scientists who study heredity—the way people pass down their physical or mental qualities from one generation to the next, from parent to child. In 1987, geneticists Allan Wilson, Rebecca Cann, and Mark Stoneking suggested that everyone on earth descended from a single African woman who lived some 200,000 years ago. In the years since, this theory has become widely accepted. So when the first European explorers reached the shores of Ghana in the 1400s and confronted the country's natives, it was in many ways a family reunion.

The *Homo sapiens* who lived thousands of years ago left behind everything from crude tools and pottery to drawings on cave walls.

The coffins of Nungua are one of Ghana's more unusual crafts. In the mid-1900s, a local chief asked woodworker Ata Owoo to build a chair for him in the shape of a giant cocoa pod. The chief died before the chair was completed, and Owoo transformed the chair into a coffin. Over fifty years later, the coffin builders of Ghana make coffins to order—in the shape of butterflies, lobsters, shoes, and even expensive cars.

Unfortunately there is little evidence from West Africa's first settlements. Near Ghana's Oti River, evidence indicates a settlement there around 12,000 years ago. Pottery discovered near the country's capital, Accra, dates to 4000 B.C.E. Iron was first used to make tools in West Africa around 500 B.C.E.

The earliest settlers in Ghana survived by hunting and gathering —they ate what they could kill or find. They were nomadic, moving often. When people began farming, they stayed in one place, forming communities. Although grain was cultivated in Egypt before 7000 B.C.E., farming did not arrive in West Africa until thousands of years later.

By around 2000 B.C.E., the Kintampo culture had introduced farming and herding to the Black Volta River region. One thousand years later, farms were well-developed, supporting everything from cattle to guinea fowl. Small communities in Ghana grew to villages of two or three thousand people.

Historians believe that by around 300 C.E., the ancient empire of Ghana had been established. Although it shares a name with the modern country, the empire was located about 500 miles (800 kilometers) north of Ghana today. Still, the empire would be an important influence to the present-day nation.

Across West Africa, communities were governed by village elders. The Ghana Empire was different. It had an emperor whose authority was enforced by a powerful army—some 200,000 warriors, mostly from the Soninke tribe. The Ghana Empire's location also helped to increase its power. Lying along a trade route between gold and ivory producers to the south and Berber merchants in the north, the empire taxed every

Camels have been used for thousands of years to transport goods and people in Ghana and beyond.

donkey or camel load which entered its borders. This was a huge source of income for the king. Another was the empire's gold mines.

Camel caravans linked North Africa with the empire. People traveled hundreds of miles to buy and sell goods. Archaeologists digging within the empire's border have uncovered coins from North Africa that were minted 1,700 years ago.

Our knowledge of the ancient empire of Ghana comes mainly from the griots. Respected members of the community, griots tell stories about the past. Part dance, part poetry, these stories entertain and inform. This form of storytelling is called an oral history, because it is spoken instead of written down. The oral histories of early West Africans blend facts and fables into a mythological soup.

Every clan and village had their own griot. So did members of the royal family. Griots acted as their personal recorders, noting births and

FYI FACT:

The rulers of the Soninke people had many titles, one of which was "warrior king" or "Ghana." Outsiders began calling both the king and the empire he ruled Ghana. The name stuck.

FYI FACT:

The actual name for the empire of Ghana was Wagadu, which was also known by three other names throughout its history: Dierra, Agada, and Silla.

deaths, celebrations and victories in battle. These stories were passed along from one generation to another as older griots taught the younger ones. This oral history was eventually written down in the *Dausi,* a collection of stories about the region's four kingdoms. In the 11th century, Abu Abdullah Al-Bakri, a Moorish nobleman who lived in Cordova, Spain, began interviewing travelers returning from West Africa. He also collected records and documents of trips to the region. Although Al-Bakri never set foot in Ghana, he described it fairly accurately in a series of books, including his best-known work, *The Book of Routes and Kingdoms.*

Trade formed ties between the nomadic Berbers and the farmers and merchants of the Ghana Empire. These bonds, however, were fairly weak. Battles often raged. Sometimes ample rainfall and healthy crops motivated the Soninke to invade Berber territory. At other times, the Berbers raided Soninke communities.

By 700 C.E., the empire's golden age had begun. However, the rise of Islam in the northern and eastern regions of Africa would help bring about the empire's downfall, and would radically change not only the empire, but much of West Africa as well.

In 1076, Islamic Berbers defeated the Soninke warriors. The Berbers' victory helped spread Islam throughout the area. Meanwhile, drought and warfare cost the empire thousands of lives. The Soninke tribe began to disperse. By 1200, some of them had settled in the area where modern Ghana is located. And by the 1400s, the lives of many West Africans would be altered by another, more powerful empire —one thousands of miles and an ocean away.

Pictured here in the 1990s, Elmina Castle was built in 1482. Today it is a popular tourist attraction, but hundreds of years ago, it held African men, women, and children as prisoners in tight quarters. They finally left through the "Door of No Return," where they were shipped to their final destinations as slaves.

Like a silent warrior, Elmina Castle looms over the Gulf of Guinea. For centuries the building has cast its shadow over the turbulent waters below. Today it is a popular tourist destination. But soon after its construction in 1482, it became a sorrowful emblem—a memorial to one of the darkest periods in the region's history.

Within its fortified walls, damp dungeons held men, women, and children who were bought and sold like cattle. The unfortunates once lived in small villages across West Africa. They were usually captured by Africans and purchased by Europeans. Bound for the New World, those who survived the rough and dangerous Atlantic crossing (for many thousands did not) faced a lifetime of hard labor.

The Europeans did not come to Ghana seeking slaves. They came for gold.

In 1415, a member of the Portuguese royal family named Prince Henry led an army that captured the city of Ceuta. This North African trading center was a favorite destination for Arab traders who brought gold from across the Sahara Desert. The gold was legendary.

Prince Henry wanted to explore Africa to find the source of the gold. In order to do this, he paid for the development of the caravel. This innovative ship was big enough for large crews and cargo, while its design and equipment—including the Chinese-developed compass for navigation—allowed it to travel great distances. Because of his explorations, he is now known as Henry the Navigator.

Prince Henry the Navigator

Although Prince Henry died in 1460, his mission lived on. Portugal sent ships south along the West Coast of Africa.

After several shorter trips, Portuguese explorers finally landed in southwestern Ghana. They named the site, *Da Costa de el Mina de Ouro,* or "The Coast of Gold Mines." For hundreds of years, the region would be better known as the "Gold Coast."

FYI FACT:

Elmina Castle was completed in 1482. Also known as St. George's Castle, it was designed to store gold and protect trading posts. A foothold in Africa for Portugal, it was the first European fort in the region.

Portugal's gold trade increased from some 8,000 ounces taken from the Gold Coast in 1489 to over 22,000 ounces each year a decade later. In the next century, Portugal began to trade for other resources, including human beings. Soon after, other European countries like Britain and France were competing with Portugal for these resources.

Africa has a long history of slavery. In battle, victorious tribes often took those they defeated as slaves. The Gold Coast's dangerous gold mines relied on slave labor.

East of Ghana, records show that slaves were captured and brought across the Sahara Desert before 650 C.E.; less than 200 years later, slaves were being shipped across the Red Sea from East Africa. Some estimates hold that in various parts of Africa during the period when Europeans were first exploring, as much as one-third of the population was enslaved.

Throughout the area now known as Ghana, the Portuguese traded goods in exchange for gold. Horses were valuable, but did not travel well. Guns were popular. But the goods the native people needed most were slaves to work in the mines and clear the forests for farms. By the early 1500s, Portuguese vessels landing on the Gold Coast held slaves captured from Benin.

Slaves who lived and worked in Africa were treated far differently than the ones enslaved by Europeans. Slaves in Africa typically were not slaves for life, and were often treated more like members of the family than as the property of their owners. Estimates suggest that in the late 1700s, around 100,000 men, women, and children were sold as slaves out of West Africa every year. Many more died trying to escape their captors in the harsh inland terrain. According to author John Reader, transporting "9 million slaves across the Atlantic between 1700 and 1850... required the capture of an estimated 21 million Africans, of whom 7 million were taken into domestic slavery [enslaved in Africa] and another 12 million died within a year of capture. The population of most of sub-Saharan Africa did not increase at all in the hundred years between 1750 and 1850."[1]

While the very old, the very weak, and the very sick were left behind, communities often lost their youngest and strongest members.

The slave trade's damage lasted long after the practice was banned. Robbed of the very people who empower countries, the regions that lost thousands to slavery had a difficult time recovering. In *Africa,* Reader explains, "The effects of the slave trade's forced migration of millions from Africa were pernicious [highly destructive], were unrelenting, and went on for more than 1,000 years."[2]

Across the world, explorers were claiming new territories. They may have been the first Europeans in places like Africa and North America, but this territory was not really discovered by them. It had already been discovered—by people who had made their homes on the land thousands of years before the Europeans arrived. People crossing the Bering Strait from Asia settled across North America long before Europeans carved it up into colonies. In Africa, as in the Americas, natives were displaced, and even killed in favor of European interests.

A view of the northwest side of Elmina Castle, from the river.

In the late 1500s, the Dutch began to battle Portugal for control of the Gold Coast. In 1637, the Dutch prevailed, seizing Elmina Castle. Five years later, the Dutch controlled the entire Gold Coast. Beginning in 1650, the Danes and the Swedes erected castles up and down the coastline, until the fortresses were only a few miles apart. But further inland, a new African empire was growing. This empire would soon challenge European powers.

FYI FACT:

Most of Ghana's population in the 1500s had migrated into the region several hundred years before. They included the Ashanti (Asante) and Fante, who left the savanna to the north and settled in central forest lands near the southern coast, and the Mandé, descendants of the Ghana Empire who left Mali for northern Ghana.

Although it was less than two feet high, The Golden Stool was believed to hold enormous power. It was even partly responsible for a major conflict, The War of the Golden Stool.

The Golden Kingdom

One of Ghana's most important national symbols is rarely seen in public. It is a stool. Two feet (61 centimeters) wide and 18 inches (46 centimeters) high, the stool is solid gold. Not only does it never touch the ground, but when a new Ashanti King is crowned, even he is not allowed to sit upon it. Instead, he is lowered and raised over it. His body never touches it.

It is said that the stool was summoned from the sky by an Ashanti priest named Okomfo Anokye. He warned his people, "if [the Golden Stool] is ever captured or destroyed, then just as a man sickens and dies without his soul, so will the Ashanti lose their power and disintegrate into chaos." Thus the Golden Stool of the Ashanti is quite literally the seat of power.[1]

Today the Akan are the largest ethnic group in Ghana. There are four main Akan tribes in the country today: the Fante, the Akuapem, the Akyem, and the Ashanti; the Ashanti are the largest in all of Ghana. In the late 1600s, the Ashanti were under the control of the most powerful Akan state of the time—Denkyira. At that time, the leader of the Ashanti died, and his power passed to his nephew, Osei Tutu.

In the late 17th century, the Ashanti were living in the area that is the modern-day city of Kumasi. Located in the Ashanti Region of Ghana, Kumasi lies at the edges of the rainforest. From there, the Ashanti harvested kola nuts, while nearby farms produced ample food. Ashanti slaves worked the gold mines.

Using Kumasi's great wealth, Tutu united the various independent chiefs against Denkyira. By 1701, the Ashanti were victorious. "Oral tradition relates that the [Golden Stool of Ashanti] came into existence around 1700," explains author Monica Visonà. "Osei Tutu had a clever priest, Anokye, whose power caused the Golden Stool, which was said to contain the spirit of the Asante nation, to appear from the sky, whereupon it fell onto the lap of Osei Tutu."[2]

Under Tutu, the Ashanti created a strong central government with the king (or *asantehene*) sharing power with a national assembly (called the *asantemanhyiamu*). This assembly was made up of senior chiefs and local rulers. Meeting once a year, they made decisions about disputes and passed laws. There was also a smaller council of some seventeen wealthy Ashanti who served as a court. Unusual for the time, women were given considerable power in the Ashanti Kingdom. The queen-mother helped to select the next king, and was an advisor to him as well. Power also passed from the mother's side of the king's family.

As Tutu's kingdom grew, the Ashanti began trading gold with the Europeans on the coast, often for slaves from other parts of Africa. They used these slaves to clear the forests for farms. They were put to work in the mines where the pits were over 160 feet (50 meters) deep. In some mines, it was reported that each miner was expected to dig up at least two ounces of gold each day. One of the largest mines employed ten thousand slaves.

Gold was not just used for trade with the Europeans. It was paid as a tribute from Ashanti's provinces and as fines for crimes (even someone facing death could buy their freedom with 500 ounces.) As more and more gold was used within the Ashanti Kingdom, less was traded with the Europeans.

By the 1700s, Europeans on the Gold Coast no longer traded slaves for gold. Instead, as the need for slaves in the New World increased, Africans were captured by groups like the Ashanti. They were then traded for things like guns and food.

In 1717, Osei Tutu died in war, but his legacy lives on through the Ashanti Empire he founded. He inherited a small kingdom, but put systems in place that enabled it to grow. The laws that he crafted were

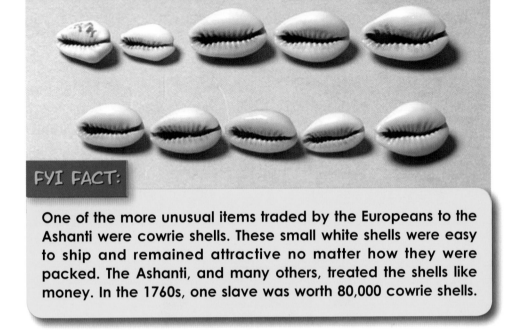

FYI FACT:

One of the more unusual items traded by the Europeans to the Ashanti were cowrie shells. These small white shells were easy to ship and remained attractive no matter how they were packed. The Ashanti, and many others, treated the shells like money. In the 1760s, one slave was worth 80,000 cowrie shells.

used in Ghana's 1959 Constitution to govern relationships between the Ashanti Regional House of Chiefs and the government of Ghana.

Despite the loss of Tutu, the empire's material wealth grew. Instead of trails, four well-maintained roads tracked from Kumasi to the savanna; another four carried goods from Kumasi south to the Atlantic Ocean. By 1820, the Ashanti Empire numbered some five million people, and reached from Kumasi to the coast. It was larger than Great Britain is today.

During the late 1700s, Britain struggled to gain power along the Gold Coast. The common phrase "the sun never sets on the British Empire," described a country with colonies across the planet. No matter what time of day or night it was in England, somewhere on earth sunlight was falling upon a territory the country controlled. At its peak, it was the largest empire in history.

The first conflicts between the British and the Ashanti began in the early 1800s, as the Ashanti looked to expand their empire. By the end of the 19th century, Britain moved to colonize the Ashanti area. Yet just as the United States declared her independence from Britain in 1776, the Ashanti battled for their own freedom in the years to follow.

Accra's Black Star Square serves as both a meeting place and a symbol of Ghanaian freedom.

Chapter 6

Independence

Overlooking the ocean, Black Star Square stands as both landmark and beacon. Also called Independence Square, it is a familiar meeting place in the capital city of Accra, while its Eternal Flame of African Liberation reminds Ghanaians of their long struggle for freedom.

In the early 1800s, two expanding empires collided. Powered by gold wealth, the Ashanti Kingdom invaded their weaker neighbors. Meanwhile, Britain took over Portuguese and Danish colonies. In Ghana, Britain controlled land near the Atlantic Ocean; Ashanti territory lay across the central part of the modern-day country. As it grew, the Ashanti Empire approached the regions under British rule. At its largest, the Ashanti Empire was more than double the size of present-day Ghana.

In 1807, a major source of Ashanti wealth was outlawed. The British Parliament made slave trading illegal. British vessels patrolling West Africa's coast began boarding ships suspected of carrying slaves. Over 100,000 enslaved Africans were freed between 1807 and 1860.

The African Company of Merchants administering the British-ruled coastal regions signed a treaty with the Ashanti accepting the empire's right to large sections of the coastline. But when the Merchants couldn't stop the Ashanti slave trade, Britain dissolved the organization. In 1821, those coastal areas became crown colonies. The country Europeans called the Gold Coast would be run by the governor of Sierra Leone, Brigadier-General Sir Charles MacCarthy. The Ashanti had other ideas.

Battle between the British and the Ashanti, 1824.

The first of nine bloody battles began in 1823. Although the British claimed the fighting was over the Ashanti slave trade, many believe the British attacked for one reason. They wanted Ashanti gold.

The First Anglo-Ashanti War began after the coastal Fante tribe, worried about an Ashanti invasion, joined British forces under Mac-Carthy's command. On opposing shores of the Pra River, the two sides met. On one shoreline, around 240 Fante warriors and 200 British soldiers waited for reinforcements. Across the river, more than 10,000 Ashanti warriors prepared to attack.

The Battle of Nsamankow didn't last long. The British ran out of ammunition, and nearly every British soldier was killed. General Mac-Carthy's skull would later be lined with gold and used as an Ashanti drinking cup.

The Ashanti victory was short-lived. British forces defeated them in 1826 during the Battle of Kantamanto. Battles continued for decades, with periods of peace in between. There were victories and defeats on both sides, until the British carried out an overwhelming attack.

"A large-scale British expedition invaded Asante in 1874," explains author Assa Okoth. "The Asante resisted the expedition's progress fiercely, but to no avail, and when the British reached Kumasi they burnt it... The Asantehene himself was dethroned soon afterwards for stealing the treasures from his ancestor's graves."[1]

As part of the the the Treaty of Fomena, the Ashanti paid the British 50,000 ounces of gold and ended alliances with Denkyira and Akyem. The weakened empire soon lost the territories of Dagomba, Brong, and Gonja as well. But one final battle awaited.

A deep misunderstanding of Ashanti traditions sparked The War of the Golden Stool. In 1900, the Gold Coast's governor, Sir Frederick Hodgson, met with the Ashanti chiefs. Hodgson believed that as the governor of the region, he should now be the one to sit on the Golden Stool. Hodgson asked, "Where is the Gold Stool? Why am I not sitting on the Golden Stool at this moment?"[2]

The Ashanti were shocked. No one—not even their king—ever sat on the stool. They didn't see it as a throne, but as the source of their power. During official ceremonies and celebrations, their king sat beside it.

Hodgson refused to believe this. He sent soldiers into Kumasi to find the stool; some of them beat Ashanti children in an effort to seize it. Enraged, the queen-mother Yaa Asantewaa led the charge. "If you the men of Ashanti will not go forward, then we will. We the women will... We will fight till the last of us falls in the battlefields."[3]

Although the Ashanti siege of the British fort in Kumasi lasted for months, it ultimately failed. The British captured Asantewaa and sent her into exile. Still, the battle became a symbol for many in the country.

In 1901, Ashanti became a British protectorate under the control of the Gold Coast Crown Colony. In many ways, the united colony was extremely successful. Chiefs were given local control, and the exiled Asantehene Prempeh I was restored to his throne in 1924. Exports of gold and cocoa grew. Roads and railroads were built; teachers were trained and the schools improved. During World Wars I and II, native Africans fought beside the British to defeat the Germans.

But after World War II, many Africans questioned why they were fighting for European freedom when they themselves were not free. In 1948, ex-servicemen marched on Accra's Christiansborg Castle with a letter for the governor seeking the benefits they were promised in exchange for their service in the wars. The police chief ordered his men to open fire. Three of the ex-servicemen were killed and six were imprisoned.

Kwame Nkrumah was one of the prisoners. After his release, he became the leader of the Convention People's Party. The organization campaigned for a new constitution and an African president under the slogan, "Self Government Now!"

Britain, still recovering from the economic damage caused by World War II, found it difficult to run colonies like the Gold Coast from thousands of miles away. Throughout the 1950s and early 1960s, many African countries worked to become independent. Ghana was the first sub-Saharan colony to achieve it.

U.S. President John F. Kennedy meets with the president of newly independent Ghana, Kwame Nkrumah, on March 8, 1961.

Numerous important dignitaries witnessed Ghana's independence ceremonies, including U.S. Vice President Richard M. Nixon and civil rights leader, Martin Luther King Jr.

In 1952, Nkrumah was elected prime minister; four years later, after winning 68 percent of the seats in the legislature, the Convention People's Party passed an independence motion. In Britain, Parliament approved.

On March 6, 1957, the former Gold Coast colony became an independent nation. Inspired by the legendary empire to the north, it was renamed Ghana.

For over forty years after gaining independence, the Republic of Ghana endured many of the same challenges faced by newly independent nations across Africa. Like many leaders of former colonies, Nkrumah was more concerned with holding onto power than with allowing the people of Ghana to choose their leader. The Preventive Detention Act of 1958 allowed his security forces to detain critics of the government for five years. He also outlawed rival political parties.

In 1966, Nkrumah was in China when a group of army officers took over the government. When people take over their government by force, it is called a coup. There would be several more major coups, including one in 1972 and one in 1979. The leader of this last coup, Flight Lieutenant Jerry Rawlings, was elected president in 1992. He ruled the country until 2001, when the constitution prevented him from running for reelection.

Following elections in 2000, John Kufuor became president. Under his leadership, the country's economy has continued to improve as many businesses that were once poorly run by the state were sold to private companies. Meanwhile, a new constitution, written in 1992 and voted on by the people, guaranteed its citizens certain rights. It also allowed political parties to form. The country's government would resemble the United States government—operating under a system with three branches: the executive, the legislative, and the judiciary.

First Lady of Ghana Ernestina Naadu Mills (left) meets United States First Lady Michelle Obama at the State Department in Washington, D.C., in March 2012

John Atta Mills meets United States President Barack Obama (right), March 2012

Like the United States, Ghana now only allows presidents to serve for two terms. The president appoints his cabinet, while the Parliament writes the laws for the country. Like the United States Congress, Ghana's Parliament is elected by the citizens. The Supreme Court was established, as it was in the United States, as an independent body which can review laws passed by the Parliament.

In 2009, John Atta Mills was elected president. The election marked the second time that power had changed hands peacefully in Ghana. Many see the elections as evidence that Ghana has finally become a stable democracy. Sadly, Mills passed away in July 2012 after battling throat cancer. His vice president John Dramani Mahama took over as interim president, and was officially elected president in December 2012.

Despite its problems politically, Ghana has had numerous successes. Exports of cocoa, timber, and gold have grown since the early years of the country's independence. It has also attracted foreign investment. One such effort led to the construction of the Akosombo Dam. While the dam flooded more than 3 percent of Ghana's land with water (now called Lake Volta), today it provides more electricity than Ghana can use, allowing the country to sell the excess to neighboring countries.

While over half of its citizens still work on farms or in other agriculture and make very little money, Ghana has a new resource. In 2007, oil was discovered near the country's coast. Estimates suggest the oil field may contain over three billion barrels of oil.

Like in many countries in Africa and across the world, soccer is Ghana's most popular sport.

Ghanaians Today

There are over one hundred ethnic groups in Ghana, each with their own dialect or language. The largest groups include the Akan (including the Ashanti and Fante), Ewe, Akyem, Dagomba, and Ga-Dangme. There are also smaller tribes throughout the country, as well as many people whose families came from other parts of the world. In rural areas, each part of the country tends to be dominated by a particular tribe. In the cities, the different groups live side by side.

The influence of the outside world is seen clearly in Ghana's religions. The most common religion is Christianity, followed by Islam, then traditional religions. Most Christian or Muslim Ghanaians blend their traditional beliefs with the religions imported by Arabs and Europeans. Historically, Muslim traders entered the country from the Sahara Desert to the north, while Europeans came by boat along the coast. Today, Christianity is most common in the south, while Islam is practiced in the north.

Traditional religious practices still play a large role in most Ghanaians' lives, as well. While these customs vary among the groups, most native religions acknowledge one supreme being. Deceased ancestors are very important, and it is believed that they can strongly influence the daily lives of the living.

Whatever their beliefs, Ghanaians are proud of their unity and are loyal to their country. One of the ways they demonstrate their unity is through football (soccer). The Ghana Black Stars have been playing since the country became independent in 1957. Fans throughout the country come together to watch games and support the team. And all that support has paid off. The Black Stars have won the Africa Cup of Nations four times (1963, 1965, 1978, and 1982), and were runners-up in 2010.

Many great football players have represented the Black Stars, but Abédi Ayew Pelé is considered the best by many. Abédi Ayew was born in a small town near Accra on November 5, 1964. At just seventeen years old, he gained fame after leading the Black Stars to a win at the Africa Cup of Nations in 1982. His talent earned him the nickname "Pelé," after the famous Brazilian football player. He went on to play for teams throughout Europe before returning to Ghana as team captain in the 1990s. Today Pelé is retired, but three of his sons, André, Ibrahim, and Jordan, play for the Black Stars.

Food is another way Ghanaians come together. Meals in Ghana usually include a starch, served with a spicy soup or stew. One of the most popular starches in Ghana is called *fufu*. Made from boiled cassava or plantains, fufu is eaten in small balls that are dipped in a stew. This dish is never chewed, only swallowed, and is always eaten with fingers, not silverware. In Ghana, the right hand should always be used for eating, as the left hand is considered unclean.

While fufu is a staple along the Ghanaian coast, *tuo zaafi* is a common dish in the north. The starch in this meal is made of corn and cassava flour, and it is usually eaten with okra stew. It is common to add meats such as goat, beef, or lamb to stews.

Many Ghanaian customs are very different from Western customs. In Ghana, if a person is eating in front of others, it is considered polite to offer to share. Whether the other people are friends or complete strangers, not offering is considered offensive. To Ghanaians, it is important to greet everyone who crosses your path, but elders should

FYI FACT:

Zetahil is a unique religion that was established in Ghana, combining elements of both Christianity and Islam.

Abédi Ayew Pelé

always be greeted first. Elders are always given the highest respect for their experience and wisdom. Personal space is another cultural difference in Ghana; a Ghanaian might stand much closer to you than an American would.

Historically, women in Ghana were discouraged from going to school and working. As children, they were often needed at home to work on the farms. It was also assumed that when they were old enough to work, their husbands would support them. Even though education was required by law in 1960, in 1990, only 39 percent of secondary school students were female. But slowly, views have changed, and by 2011, that number had risen to 46 percent.[1]

Today, 67 percent of women over the age of fifteen are working in Ghana.[2] But women still face the challenges of discrimination in the professional world.

Akua Kuenyehia is one woman who was able to overcome these challenges. Kuenyehia realized the importance of education from a young age, and worked hard to earn her law degree. Today, she is a

Today, more and more young women in Ghana are pursuing higher education. Akua Kuenyehia earned her law degree at a time when most attorneys were men. Today, she is an International Criminal Court judge.

judge for the International Criminal Court in the Netherlands. From 2003 to 2009, she served as the first vice-president of the Court. In addition to her work as a judge, she also fights for gender equality in Ghana and around the world. "If we are to make progress in our developmental efforts as a nation then we ought to find ways of accelerating female education, because no nation can move forward with only half of its population," she said.[3] Kuenyehia feels it is important to give back, and she helps girls receive the education they need to become successful.

One of the most famous Ghanaian writers is also a woman. Ama Ata Aidoo was born in 1942 to a royal Fante family. Her father sent her to school and encouraged her dreams—at fifteen she knew she wanted to be a writer. Four years later she won a competition and was on her way. She penned the plays *The Dilemma of a Ghost* and *Anowa,* but she is best known for *No Sweetness Here,* a collection of short stories. Most of her work addresses the challenges faced by African women. She also writes about the differences between Western and African cultures and beliefs.

In 2012, noted author Ama Ata Aidoo released her latest work, a collection of short stories entitled *Diplomatic Pounds & Other Stories.*

Ghana celebrates Independence Day every year on March 6 with a parade of music, dance, and military formations. Some 30,000 spectators show up to experience the festivities.

Cities, Sights, and Celebrations!

The diversity of cultures and rich history of Ghana make it an exciting place to visit. From nature reserves to beaches, markets to castles, and hand-made crafts to festivals, Ghana has something to offer every visitor.

Ghana's capital city of Accra is a modern city with a population of over two million people. Black Star Square (or Independence Square) can be found near the coast of the city. The square is home to the largest Independence Day ceremony in the country. Just as the United States celebrates its independence on July 4, Ghana celebrates its independence on March 6 each year. The festivities at Black Star Square include a parade of military and police officers, music and dance. It is estimated that over 30,000 people attend the event every year.

Founder's Day is another national holiday that is celebrated throughout Ghana. On September 21, this day honors the birthday of Kwame Nkrumah, the first prime minister of the independent country. Educated in the United States, Nkrumah returned to the Gold Coast in 1949 and organized the Convention People's Party. Although he was later forcibly removed as prime minister, he is recognized for his contributions to the history of Ghana.

These contributions can be witnessed today at Kwame Nkrumah Memorial Park in Accra. Aside from being the burial place of the leader, a museum in his honor holds many of his personal belongings here. Details of his life history are on display alongside photos of

Ghana's capital city of Accra offers many tourist attractions, including Kwame Nkrumah Memorial Park. The mausoleum of the country's first president is located on the park's grounds.

Nkrumah with other world leaders like John F. Kennedy, Queen Elizabeth II, and Fidel Castro.

The Ga-Dangme people are one of the largest groups located in the Accra Region. Each year, they celebrate the harvest of the new year with the Homowo Festival. The people say that this festival began in a time of famine. There was a drought in the area, but the people worked hard to grow their crops. When they finally were able to harvest their food, they celebrated with *homowo,* or "making fun of hunger."

The Ga-Dangme use their own calendar, so the festival can take place any time from July to September. Preparations for the festival begin a month in advance: drumming and loud noises are prohibited, and on certain days farmers are not allowed to work. The festival is held on a Saturday, the thirteenth day of the new year. The royal family receives blessings and meals from the priest to protect them from evil. Warriors participate in boat races, and the chief scatters food on the ground as an offering to the gods. People dressed in bright colors parade down the streets singing, dancing, and playing instruments.

Across the coast of Ghana, forts and castles stand as reminders of the European presence in the country. Today, visitors tour the buildings where thousands of slaves were kept, waiting to be shipped to the Americas. Elmina Castle and Cape Coast Castle are popular among tourists interested in learning more about Ghana's history.

Panafest is another way visitors can learn about the history of Ghana. Held in July each year, this event showcases modern African dance and theater, but also takes attendees on a tour of the country to visit important historic and cultural sites. The effects of slavery are a focus of the tour, which usually includes sites in the north, as well as the coastal castles.

Dance is a vital part of Ghana's past and its present. Here a modern dance performer offers an interpretation of an Akan symbol that represents the oneness of God.

The second-largest city in Ghana is the former Ashanti capital of Kumasi. Lying about 150 miles (250 kilometers) northwest of Accra, over 1.7 million people reside in Kumasi today. Hundreds of years ago, Kumasi was a major trading point; today it is home to the Kejetia Market, the largest open-air market in West Africa. Here, bustling crowds include locals buying fruits and vegetables, and tourists shopping for everything from clothes and metal crafts to dried snake skins and shrunken monkey heads. In Ghanaian culture, bargaining is part of the shopping experience. Vendors start with high prices, knowing that the customer will expect to pay half of the asking price, or even less. The market is the perfect place to practice your negotiating skills!

The largest open-air market in West Africa, the Kejetia Market offers shoppers everything from fruits to shrunken monkey heads!

Born in Kumasi, Kofi Atta Annan is a descendant of tribal chiefs. Annan attended college in the United States, earning a bachelor's degree at Minnesota's Macalester College and a master's degree at the Massachusetts Institute of Technology. His work at the United Nations led him to become the secretary-general of the U.N., the first black African to hold that position.

The Ashanti today hold one of the most elaborate festivals in the country: the Adae Kese. This celebration marks the Ashantis' major milestones; the first one was held in 1701 when the Ashanti defeated the Denkyira to become an independent state. Before the public displays, the Asantehene eats a special meal dedicated to the ancestors. This meal is believed to cleanse and purify the king's soul. The king prays to the ancestors for their help and protection for the entire kingdom. The king then leads a parade with his chiefs, and the people join in. Dressed in clothing made from kente cloth, and *ahenema* sandals, the Ashanti carry umbrellas down the streets, dancing, drumming, and singing. While the Adae Kese is held only on special occasions, visitors can often enjoy a smaller version of the festival. The Akwasidae is held at the beginning of each new *adaduanan* (month)—which comes around every forty-two days in the Ashanti calendar.

Ghanaian Recipe

Fufu

This traditional Ghanaian dish is as much fun to make as it is to eat, maybe more so! **You will need an adult to help prepare this dish.** Usually made with plantains or cassava, this recipe uses products found in many American kitchens.

You will need:
2 ½   cups of Bisquick
2 ½   cups of instant potato flakes
6   cups of water
      A large pot
      A wooden spoon
      Two bowls (one slightly moistened)

1. Bring the water to a rapid boil in the pot.
2. While you wait for the water to boil, mix the Bisquick and instant potato flakes in a bowl.
3. Once the water is boiling, add the contents of the bowl.
4. One person should stir while the other holds the pot. This will take a lot of strength as the mixture thickens.
5. After about 10 to 15 minutes, when the mixture is difficult to stir, scoop out 1 cup and place it in the wet bowl. Shake the bowl until the mixture becomes a ball. Repeat with the rest of the mixture.
6. Serve on a plate accompanied by a stew.

Ghanaian Craft

Kente

Kente means "basket." Kente is a cloth with a weave that resembles a basket. The weaving of kente cloth originated in the 11th century with the Akan people. Once worn only by royalty, kente has been worn not only by many in Ghana, but after President Kwame Nkrumah brought a kente-wearing entourage to the U.S., Americans began to imitate the fashion. The "kente" jackets and dresses in the 1960s United States were controversial, however, because they were not hand-made.

This craft is a good way to learn about kente cloth and what its colors mean: blue usually is a color of love and harmony. Black symbolizes maturity or mourning, while gold symbolizes fertility, royalty, or monetary wealth. Green can represent the land, or spiritual growth and renewal, while yellow is the color of royalty or high worth. Grey is for healing rituals, while pink is a feminine color, and white is for purity. Red is used for funerals, while silver is the color of peace.

You will need:
A pair of scissors
A ruler
Thick white paper—like construction paper
Markers
Tape
Poster board
Some pictures of kente cloth

1. Begin by using the ruler to draw straight lines horizontally across a sheet of paper. Each line should be about the width of a ruler.
2. Using the pictures as a guide, color in the strips with patterns.
3. Cut the strips along the lines.
4. Fold a separate sheet of paper in half horizontally. Then, using the scissors, cut vertically across the fold. Each cut should be about ruler-width apart, and almost (but not quite) to the end of the paper. Unfold.
5. Color this paper with different patterns.
6. Now "weave" the strips of paper into the cuts you have made. Alternate so that where the first strip of paper goes underneath the cut, the second will go over it.
7. When you are done, tape the paper to a thick piece of cardboard or poster board for display.

TIMELINE

B.C.E.

10,000   The first settlements are built along the shores of the Oti River.

4000   Pottery is created in the area near Ghana's capital city, Accra.

2000   The Kintampo people build settlements near the Black Volta River, relying on farming and herding for food—the first in the region to do so.

500   The Iron Age begins in West Africa, as people there craft tools from iron.

C.E.

ca. 300   The Empire of Ghana is established.

1068   Abu Abdullah Al-Bakri describes West Africa in *The Book of Routes and Kingdoms.*

1076   Berbers defeat the warriors of Ghana, resulting in the eventual downfall of the empire.

1200   Early migrations from Gonja begin, moving south along the Volta Basin to the Gulf of Guinea.

ca. 1300   Founding of the Akan Kingdom of Bono (or Brong); other states begin to develop nearby.

1471   Arrival of the Portuguese, the first Europeans to explore Ghana.

1482   The Portuguese construct Elmina Castle.

1500-1807   The Gold Coast region including Ghana is a primary source of slaves during this period.

1642   After battling the Portuguese since the late 1500s, The Dutch have established control of the entire Gold Coast.

1700   The Ashanti Golden Stool comes into existence.

1701   The Ashanti Empire wins independence from Denkyira; later becomes the region's strongest native power.

1717   Osei Tutu, the Ashanti king, is killed in battle.

1807   British Parliament outlaws the slave trade.

1820   Peak of the Ashanti Empire.

1821   Coastal areas of the Gold Coast become colonies of Britain, run by Sir Charles MacCarthy.

1823-1824   The first of nine major battles is fought over territory and independence from Britain.

1826   The Battle of Kantamanto ends with Ashanti defeat.

1831	A peace treaty signed by the British gives the Ashanti the right to unrestricted trade for six years, in exchange for 600 ounces of gold.
1863	The Ashantis defeat the British in the Battle of Bobikuma.
1874	The final invasion of coastal territories by the British ends with Ashanti defeat after the British capture Kumasi.
1876	Cocoa beans are introduced to the Gold Coast by Tetteh Quarshie.
1888	Prempeh I is crowned king of the Ashanti Kingdom.
1896	British troops seize Kumasi during the Anglo-Ashanti War and exile King Prempeh I.
1900	The colony's Legislative Council accepts the first African members; after the British demand the Golden Stool, queen-mother Yaa Asantewaa leads an attack on the British in Kumasi.
1901	Britain declares the Ashanti areas a British protectorate.
1922	Following World War I, adjoining territory of Togoland becomes a British protectorate.
1924	King Prempeh I returns to Ghana.
1925	New Constitution calls for six chiefs to be elected to Legislative Council
1952	Kwame Nkrumah is elected prime minister of the Gold Coast, and begins to work towards independence.
1957	On March 6, Ghana becomes independent.
1960	The new government passes laws making education free and compulsory.
1963	Independent Ghana's football team, the Black Stars, wins its first Africa Cup of Nations.
1966	Nkrumah is overthrown in a coup.
1981	Jerry Rawlings leads a group that overthrows the government; he is elected president in 1992, and remains in power until 2001.
1992	A new constitution protects the rights of the citizens of Ghana, and allows for opposing political parties.
2000	John Kufuor is elected president.
2007	A three-billion-barrel oil field is discovered off the coast of Ghana.
2009	John Atta Mills becomes president after Kufuor serves two terms.
2012	Mills passes away after battling throat cancer; Vice President John Dramani Mahama wins presidential election.

Chapter 2. Where the Wild Things Are

1. John Reader, *Africa: A Biography of the Continent* (New York: Alfred A. Knopf, 1998), pp. 33-34.

2. *United Nations Convention to Combat Desertification,* "Combating desertification in Africa: Fact Sheet 11," updated January 24, 2008, http://www.unccd.int/Lists/SiteDocumentLibrary/Publications/Fact_sheet_11eng.pdf

3. S.O. Saaka Abdullah Iddrisu and Edward M. Telly, "National Report to the Third Session of the Conference of the Parties to the United Nations Convention to Combat Desertification," Republic of Ghana, May 1999.

4. Ibid.

Chapter 4. Europeans Arrive

1. John Reader, *Africa* (Washington, D.C.: National Geographic, 2001), p. 259.

2. Ibid.

Chapter 5. The Golden Kingdom

1. John Reader, *Africa: A Biography of the Continent* (New York: A.A. Knopf, 1998), p. 424.

2. Monica Blackmun Visonà, *A History of Art in Africa* (New York: Harry N. Abrams, 2001), p. 198.

Chapter 6. Independence

1. Assa Okoth, *A History of Africa: African Societies and the Establishment of Colonial Rule* (Nairobi: East African Educational Publishers, 2006), p. 20.

2. BBC World Service, "Asante," *The Story of Africa: West African Kingdoms,* http://www.bbc.co.uk/worldservice/africa/features/storyofafrica/4chapter6.shtml

3. Ivan Van Sertima, ed., *Black Women in Antiquity* (New Brunswick, NJ: Transaction Publishers, 1988), p. 133.

Chapter 7. Ghanaians Today

1. The World Bank, "Ghana," http://data.worldbank.org/country/ghana

2. Ibid.

3. Akua Kuenyehia Foundation, "Message From Akua Kuenyehia," http://www.akuakuenyehiafoundation.com/msg.htm

Books

Brace, Steve. *Ghana*. New York: Thomson Learning, 1995.

La Pierre, Yvette. *Ghana in Pictures*. Minneapolis: Lerner Publications Co., 2004.

Levy, Patricia, and Winnie Wong. *Ghana*. New York: Marshall Cavendish, 2010.

Oppong, Joseph R., and Esther D. Oppong. *Ghana*. Philadelphia: Chelsea House Publishers, 2003.

Ross, Stewart, and Stephen Biesty. *Into the Unknown: How Great Explorers Found Their Way by Land, Sea, and Air*. Somerville, Mass.: Candlewick Press, 2011.

On the Internet

BBC News: "Ghana Profile," *Africa*
http://www.bbc.co.uk/news/world-africa-13433790

Castles and Forts in Ghana
http://www.castles.nl/gh/gh.html

GhanaWeb
http://www.ghanaweb.com/GhanaHomePage/

National Geographic Kids: "Ghana"
http://kids.nationalgeographic.com/kids/places/find/ghana/

Out to Africa with Ellen and Paul: "Hyrax"
http://www.outtoafrica.nl/animals/enghyrax.html?zenden=2&subsoort_id=4&bestemming_id=1

U.S. Department of State: "U.S. Relations With Ghana"
http://www.state.gov/r/pa/ei/bgn/2860.htm

WORKS CONSULTED

Africa Travel Magazine, Western Africa Edition: "Ghana Tour Photos." http://www.africa-ata.org/gh_photos4.htm

Akua Kuenyehia Foundation: "Message From Akua Kuenyehia." http://www.akuakuenyehiafoundation.com/msg.htm

BBC World Service: "Ama Ata Aidoo," *Women Writers*. http://www.bbc.co.uk/worldservice/arts/features/womenwriters/aidoo_life.shtml

BBC World Service: "Asante," *The Story of Africa: West African Kingdoms*. http://www.bbc.co.uk/worldservice/africa/features/storyofafrica/4chapter6.shtml

Briggs, Phillip. *Ghana*. Chalfont St. Peter, England: Bradt Travel Guides, 2010.

Central Intelligence Agency: "Ghana," *The World Factbook*. https://www.cia.gov/library/publications/the-world-factbook/geos/gh.html

DeWolf, Thomas Norman. *Inheriting the Trade: A Northern Family Confronts its Legacy as the Largest Slave-Trading Dynasty in U.S. History*. Boston: Beacon Press, 2008.

"Elmina Castle," YouTube Video, uploaded by "rijn42" on September 30, 2009. http://www.youtube.com/watch?v=Dg6kQKlZzcg

Ghana Embassy. http://www.ghanaembassy.org/

GhanaToGhana.com, "Abedi Pele Biography," April 18, 2011. http://www.ghanatoghana.com/Ghanahomepage/abedi-pele-biography-view-information-abedi-pele-ghana

Ghana Tourism: "Mole National Park." http://www.touringghana.com/ecotourism/mole.asp

"Ghana: Tourist Attractions," YouTube video, uploaded by SuperShark80 on October 5, 2008. http://www.youtube.com/watch?v=RmbTwFOmFzg

Go Travel Ghana: "Kakum National Park Canopy Walk." http://gotravelghana.com/kakum-national-park-canopy-walk/

Hewitt, Andrew. "Christmas and New Year's in Ghana," TravelBlog. http://www.travelblog.org/Africa/Ghana/Ashanti/Akrokerri/blog-464317.html

Iddrisu, S.O. Saaka Abdullah, and Edward M. Telly. "National Report to the Third Session of the Conference of the Parties to the United Nations Convention to Combat Desertification." Republic of Ghana, May 1999.

International Criminal Court: "Judge Akua Kuenyehia (Ghana)." http://www.icc-cpi.int/Menus/ICC/Structure+of+the+Court/Chambers/The+Judges/The+Judges/Judge+Akua+Kuenyehia/

"Kakum National Park Canopy Walk—Scared of Heights?" YouTube video, uploaded by Jiglet on November 6, 2008. http://youtu.be/oAYnivamaJ4

Karlya, Maria, et. al. *Ghana*. Durham, NC: Other Places Publishing, 2012.

Kay Sports Magazine. "Abedi Ayew Pele." vol. 1, January 2008, pp. 39-40.

Kwintessential: "Ghana—Language, Culture, Customs, and Etiquette." http://www.kwintessential. co.uk/resources/global-etiquette/ghana.html

Makina, Adan. "The impacts of black and white slavery and the legacy of imperialism and colonialism on the African continent." http://www.wardheernews.com/Articles_09/May/Adan_Makina/The%20impacts%20of%20black%20and%20white%20slavery%20and%20the%20legacies%20of%20imperialism%20and%20colonialism%20on%20the%20African%20continent[1].pdf

McKissack, Pat, and Fredrick McKissack. *The Royal Kingdoms of Ghana, Mali, and Songhay.* New York: Henry Holt and Company, 1994.

National Geographic: "Ghana Guide." http://travel.nationalgeographic.com/travel/countries/ghana-guide/

National Geographic: "Mole National Park," Travel Favorites. http://travel.nationalgeographic.com/favorites/ghana/mole-national-park/reviews/805/

Okoth, Assa. *A History of Africa.* Nairobi: East African Educational Publishers, 2006.

OnWar.com, "Second Ashanti War 1873-1874," Wars of the World. http://www.onwar.com/aced/data/alpha/asante1873.htm

Panafest. http://www.panafestghana.org/index.php

Reader, John. *Africa: A Biography of the Continent.* New York: Alfred A. Knopf, 1998.

Reader, John. *Africa.* Washington, D.C.: National Geographic Society, 2001.

The Metropolitan Museum of Art: "The Empires of the Western Sudan: Ghana Empire," Heilbrunn Timeline of Art History. http://www.metmuseum.org/toah/hd/ghan/hd_ghan.htm

The Robinson Library: "A Timeline of Agricultural Developments." http://www.robinsonlibrary.com/agriculture/agriculture/history/timeline.htm

The World Bank: "Ghana." http://data.worldbank.org/country/ghana

United Nations Convention to Combat Desertification: "Combating desertification in Africa: Fact Sheet 11," updated January 24, 2008. http://www.unccd.int/Lists/SiteDocumentLibrary/Publications/Fact_sheet_11eng.pdf

Van Sertima, Ivan, ed. *Black Women in Antiquity.* New Brunswick, NJ: Transaction Publishers, 1988.

Visonà, Monica Blackmun. *A History of Art in Africa.* New York: Harry N. Abrams, 2001.

"West African Rainforest 'Kakum National Park,'" YouTube video, uploaded by jrincali2008 on April 2, 2009. http://youtu.be/D7Dr8LQ9sEU

Yergin, Daniel, and Joseph Stanislaw. *The Commanding Heights.* New York: Simon & Schuster, 1998.

GLOSSARY

archaeologist (ar-kee-OL-uh-jist): a scientist who studies the history and prehistory of people.

coup (KOO): a sudden takeover of power by force

craton (KRAY-ton): a stable portion of the earth's crust.

geneticist (juh-NET-uh-sist): a scientist who studies how traits are passed on from one generation to the next.

griot (GREE-oh): a person responsible for telling stories of the oral history of his or her tribe.

hominid (HAH-muh-nid): the classification of primates that stand and move on two feet, such as humans, gorillas, and chimpanzees

Homo sapiens (HOH-moh SEY-pee-uns): the species of primates to which modern human beings belong

nomad (NOH-mad): a person with no fixed home who moves from place to place.

Born in Boston, Massachusetts, John Bankston began writing articles while still a teenager. Since then, over two hundred of his articles have been published in magazines and newspapers across the country, including travel articles in *The Tallahassee Democrat*, *The Orlando Sentinel*, and *The Tallahassean*. He is the author of over sixty biographies for young adults, including works on Alexander the Great, scientist Stephen Hawking, author F. Scott Fitzgerald and actor Jodi Foster. At sixteen he enjoyed his first experience with overseas adventure, visiting Italy for two weeks with his sophomore Latin class. He currently lives in Newport Beach, California where he endures Southern California's version of Ghana's Harmattan—the Santa Ana winds. Bringing dust, pollution, and hot, dry air from the inland regions, these winds are strongest in late winter.